THE TRUTH ABOUT
JERUSALEM IN BIBLE PROPHECY

THOMAS ICE AND TIMOTHY DEMY

HARVEST HOUSE PUBLISHERS
Eugene, Oregon 97402

Scripture quotations are taken from the New American Standard Bible, © 1960, 1962, 1963, 1968, 1971, 1972, 1973, 1975, 1977 by The Lockman Foundation. Used by permission.

Cover design by Left Coast Design, Portland, Oregon

All views expressed are solely the individual authors' and do not reflect the position of any governmental agency or department.

THE TRUTH ABOUT JERUSALEM IN BIBLE PROPHECY

Copyright © 1996 by Pre-Trib Research Center
Published by Harvest House Publishers
Eugene, Oregon 97402

ISBN 1-56507-485-8

All rights reserved. No portion of this book may be reproduced in any form without the written permission of the Publisher.

Printed in the United States of America.

96 97 98 99 00 01 02 /LP/ 10 9 8 7 6 5 4 3 2 1

Contents

Introduction 7

PART 1

What Is the History of Jerusalem During the Old Testament Era?

1. *Where in the Bible do we first read of Jerusalem?* 9
2. *When did the Jews first occupy the city?* 9
3. *How did King David relate to the city?* 9
4. *Why was the First Temple built in Jerusalem?* 9
5. *What happened to Jerusalem after Solomon's reign?* .. 10

PART 2

What Is the History of Jerusalem During the New Testament Era?

6. *How did Jerusalem come under Roman control?* ... 11
7. *What was the significance of the city in the life of Jesus?* .. 12
8. *What did Jesus prophesy about Jerusalem?* 13
9. *Why was Jerusalem destroyed in A.D. 70?* 13

PART 3

What Is the History of Jerusalem After the First Century?

10. *What happened to the city during the early centuries of Christianity?* 15
11. *When did Jerusalem come under Muslim control?* .. 18
12. *Why was Jerusalem important during the Crusades?* .. 19
13. *What happened to Jerusalem in the last few centuries?* ... 20

PART 4

What Is the History of Jerusalem in the Present Century?

14. *How did Jerusalem come under British control?* ... 20
15. *What happened to Jerusalem when the state of Israel was created in 1948?* 20
16. *What happened to Jerusalem during "The Six-Day War"?* .. 21
17. *Is the current Israeli presence a fulfillment of biblical prophecy?* 21
18. *How should Christians today view Jerusalem?* 21
19. *What are some of the major prophetic passages relating to Jerusalem?* 22

PART 5

What Is the Future of Jerusalem in the Tribulation?

20. *Will Jerusalem be a city of peace or a city of war during this period?* 25
21. *How does the Antichrist relate to the city?* 26
22. *What about the rebuilding of the temple in Jerusalem?* .. 26

23. What is the relationship of the "Two Witnesses" of
    Revelation 11 to the city? 27
24. How does a revived Babylon affect the city? 27
25. What impact will the battle of Armageddon have on
    the city? 28

PART 6

What Is the Relationship of Jerusalem to the Second Coming?

26. Where does the Bible teach that Jesus will return to
    the Mount of Olives? 29
27. Is the second coming different from the rapture? ... 29
28. Why does Christ return to Jerusalem instead of some
    other city? 30

PART 7

What Is the Future of Jerusalem in the Millennium?

29. What are the physical characteristics of the city
    during this time? 30
30. What are the spiritual characteristics of the city
    during this time? 32
31. What are the political characteristics of the city
    during this time? 34
32. What happens to the city at the end of the millennium? .. 34

PART 8

What Is the Future of Jerusalem in the Eternal State?

33. Why will the city continue to exist? 35
34. What will be the size of the New Jerusalem? 35
35. Will Jerusalem be an "earthly" city or a "heavenly"
    city during eternity? 37
36. Will there be other cities as well? 37

PART 9

Why Does This Matter Today?

37. How do the prophecies concerning Jerusalem affect
    my daily life? 38
38. How should I pray for Jerusalem and the Middle East? .. 39
39. Should or can Christians be Zionists? 39
40. Isn't this really all just speculation? 40
    Conclusion 40
    Appendix: Is the Heavenly Jerusalem present during
    the millennium? 41
    A Brief Chronology of Jerusalem 43
    Notes 45

About this series...

The Pocket Prophecy series is designed to provide readers a brief summary of individual topics and issues in Bible prophecy. For quick reference and ease in studying, the works are written in a question and answer format. The questions follow a logical progression so that those reading straight through will receive a greater appreciation for the topic and the issues involved. The volumes are thorough, though not exhaustive, and can be used as a set or as single-volume studies. Each title is fully documented and contains a bibliography for further reading.

The theological perspective presented throughout the series is that of premillennialism and pretribulationism. As authors, we recognize that this is not the only position embraced by evangelical Christians, but we believe it is the most widely-held and prominent perspective. It is also our conviction that premillennialism, and specifically pretribulationism, *best* explains the prophetic plan of God as revealed in the Bible.

The study of prophecy and its puzzling pieces is an endeavor which is detailed and complex, but not beyond comprehension or resolution. It is open to error, misinterpretation, and confusion. Such possibilities should not, however, cause any Christian to shy away from either the study of prophecy or engagement in honest and helpful discussions about it. The goal of this series is to provide all those who desire to better understand the Scriptures with a concise and consistent tool. If you will do the digging the rewards will be great, and the satisfaction will remain with you as you grow in your knowledge and love of our Lord Jesus Christ and His Word.

Other books by
Thomas Ice and Timothy J. Demy

When the Trumpet Sounds
The Truth About the Rapture
The Truth About the Antichrist and His Kingdom
The Truth About the Tribulation
The Truth About the Last Days' Temple
The Truth About the Millennium
The Truth About A.D. 2000 and Predicting Christ's Return
The Coming Cashless Society

INTRODUCTION

When people think of the great cities of the world it is usually names such as Paris, Rome, London, Tokyo, and New York that come to mind. In a "top five" list, Jerusalem would probably not be cited. Yet, almost daily it seems as though the collective eyes of the world turn toward Jerusalem as headlines change, cultures clash, and diplomats debate new formulas for lasting global peace.

Jerusalem is not an economic center like New York or Tokyo. It will not rival the fashion world of Paris. It cannot offer visitors the splendor of Rome, or the treasures of London's British Museum. Jerusalem has none of the traits of the other great cities of the world. Indeed, its importance is not to be found in the realm of the secular, but rather in its spiritual significance.

The city is sacred to three of the world's religions: Judaism, Christianity, and Islam. Each religion has strong ties to the city and sacred sites within it. Yet even religious allegiance does not give Jerusalem its greatest importance. *Ultimately, the glory of Jerusalem is not found in human ascription but in divine declaration.*

Jerusalem is important because God has decreed its significance! He has declared in the Bible that it will have not only earthly significance, but also eternal significance. Of all the world's great cities, past, present, and future, only Jerusalem will be eternal. Only Jerusalem can claim a divine guarantee of perpetuity.

The Bible has more than 800 references to Jerusalem (not to mention scores of additional references by synonym), and more than 350 of these are prophetic passages relating to the future of this holy city. The pages of biblical prophecy abound with references to Jerusalem. The history, significance, and struggles of this city can be brought into focus only through the lens of Scripture. Only through the understanding of Jerusalem's prophetic role in history and the divine drama of the ages can we truly comprehend the magnitude of what we read and see each day in the news. Biblical prophecy confirms to us that Jerusalem will continue to attract global attention.

The Bible tells us that Israel and specifically Jerusalem is the center of the earth, most likely because she is at the center of God's heart and plan. Ezekiel said, "Thus says the Lord God, 'This is Jerusalem; *I have set her at the center of the nations,* with lands around her'" (Ezekiel 5:5). Later

Ezekiel speaks of Beth-togarmah coming from "the remote parts of the north" (38:6) to invade Jerusalem and the people of Israel "who live at the center of the world" (38:12).

On ancient maps, Jerusalem was placed at the center of the map, signifying that it was the geographic center of human activity. It has been common in history to refer to Israel as the center of the earth; Jerusalem the center of Israel; Mt. Zion the center of Jerusalem; and further, the Temple as Zion's center—the navel of the earth. It is not surprising to hear the Lord say in Zechariah 2:8 concerning Zion (i.e., Jerusalem), "for he who touches you, touches the apple of His eye."

Located at 31 degrees 47 minutes north latitude, 35 degrees 14 minutes east longitude, Jerusalem no longer occupies the center of the cartographer's maps and efforts. It does however remain at the center of biblical prophecy. The dynamic story of this glorious city continues today. History proclaims its past. Headlines proclaim its present. Prophecy proclaims its future.

PART 1

What Is the History of Jerusalem During the Old Testament Era?

1. Where in the Bible do we first read of Jerusalem?

In Genesis 14:18 we read that Melchizedek king of Salem brought out bread and wine and blessed Abraham. Salem was a precursor to Jerusalem (see Psalm 76:2). It was also to the adjoining hill of Moriah that Abraham later returned to offer Isaac as a sacrifice to God (Genesis 22:2). Egyptian texts from 1900–1800 B.C. refer to the Canaanite city as Urushalim. During the period of the conquest (ca. 1400 B.C.) it was known as Jebus (Judges 19:10,11; 1 Chronicles 11:4,5).

2. When did the Jews first occupy the city?

It was under the leadership of David, who became king in 1011 B.C., that the Israelites conquered the Jebusite fortress which would become Jerusalem (2 Samuel 5:6-9; 1 Chronicles 11:5,7). David's conquest was in 1004 B.C.[1]

3. How did King David relate to the city?

When David conquered Jerusalem (sometimes called Zion) he transferred his residence to it and named it after himself, "the city of David" (2 Samuel 5:9). He built up the city, and brought the ark of the Covenant to it (2 Samuel 6:12), thus making Jerusalem a center of religious worship as well as a political and military center. In doing so, David became the founder of Jerusalem.

4. Why was the First Temple built in Jerusalem?

Shortly before his death, David purchased the site of the threshing floor of Araunah the Jebusite so that an altar could be erected on it (2 Samuel 24:18-25). According to 2 Chronicles 3:1-2, it was here on Mount Moriah that Solomon began construction of the temple in 966 B.C. The building of the temple took seven years (1 Kings 6:37-38) and during this time the walls around Jerusalem were extended to encompass the temple (1 Kings 3:1).

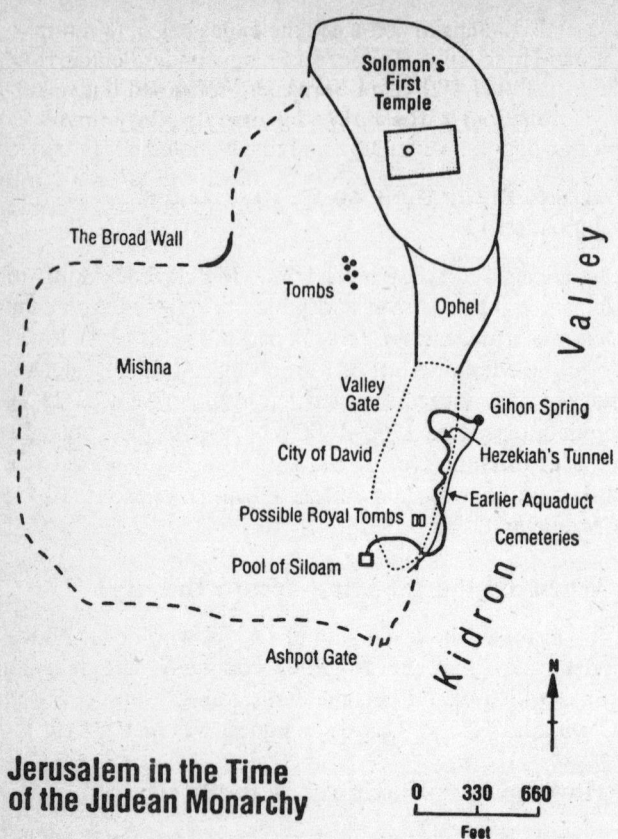

Jerusalem in the Time of the Judean Monarchy

0   330   660
Feet

5. What happened to Jerusalem after Solomon's reign?

After the death of Solomon in 931 B.C., Jerusalem went into a long period of decline. The kingdom divided and ~~Jeru~~salem became the capital of Judah only. Within five ~~year~~s of Solomon's death the temple and palace were plun~~de~~red by Egyptian troops (1 Kings 14:25-26). In the next two centuries, Jerusalem was again ransacked several times by various forces. During the reign of Uzziah from 792–740 B.C., the city was fortified (2 Chronicles 26:9-15), but after the fall of the Northern kingdom of Israel to the Assyrians in 722 B.C., Jerusalem's years were numbered.

In 597 B.C. the Babylonian ruler Nebuchadnezzar captured Jerusalem, then in 587 B.C., he destroyed both the city and the temple (2 Kings 25:8-9). After this, the city lay desolate. After the fulfillment of the prophecy of the 70 years captivity (calculated from the first submission of Jerusalem to the Babylonians in 605 B.C.), the exiles began to return to Jerusalem in 538 B.C. (Daniel 9:25), now under Persian rule.

For just over 200 years, Jerusalem remained under Persian domination. It was during this time that the temple was rebuilt in 535 B.C. (Ezra 3:8), and that Nehemiah returned to Jerusalem and rebuilt the walls of the city (444/43 B.C.). It is also at this time that the "70 weeks" of Daniel 9:24 began in 444 B.C.[2]

From 322 B.C. until 165 B.C., Jerusalem was under Greek domination, conquered first by Alexander the Great and then by his successors, the Ptolemies, and finally, by Antiochus and Antiochus IV (Antiochus Epiphanes). It was under Antiochus Epiphanes that Jerusalem was reduced to its lowest point religiously. He plundered the Second Temple and desecrated it by sacrificing a pig on the altar and fulfilling the prophecies of Daniel 11:21-35.

In 167 B.C. a priest named Matthias began a revolt against the Greek rule of the Jews. When he died, his son Judas the Maccabee continued the fight and won four successive victories against the Greeks. This struggle culminated in his reoccupation of Jerusalem and the temple in December 165 B.C. It is celebrated in an eight-day feast of dedication (Hanukkah, cf. John 10:22). Jerusalem was refortified and for just over a hundred years, it remained a free city. Yet, even during this period, there were repeated attempts to retake the city.

PART 2

What is the History of Jerusalem During the New Testament Era?

6. How did Jerusalem come under Roman control?

The fall of the free Jewish state under Hasmonean rule came in 63 B.C. when the Roman general Pompey besieged the city for three months, killed 12,000 Jews, and dismantled the walls. The Romans entered the city again in 54 B.C., and in 40 B.C., the Parthians from Persia plundered the city.

In 37 B.C. the Romans placed Herod (Herod the Great) as king over Judea, which he ruled until 4 B.C. It was under his rule that Jesus was born (Matthew 2:13; Luke 1:5). Upon Herod's death, his son Archelaus ruled Jerusalem until A.D. 6, after which it was ruled by Roman procurators from A.D. 6–41 and A.D. 44–46. It was under the fifth of these, Pontius Pilate (A.D. 26–36) that Jesus was crucified.

7. What was the significance of the city in the life of Jesus?

Jerusalem was very important in the life and ministry of Jesus. Biblical prophecy had recorded that in Jerusalem the event known as the triumphal entry would occur. Zechariah 9:9 foretold the event.

> Rejoice greatly, O daughter of Zion! Shout *in triumph,* O daughter of Jerusalem! Behold, your king is coming to you; He is just and endowed with salvation, Humble, and mounted on a donkey, Even on a colt, the foal of a donkey.

This prophecy, along with prophecies pertaining to Daniel's "70 weeks," were fulfilled down to the exact day.[3]

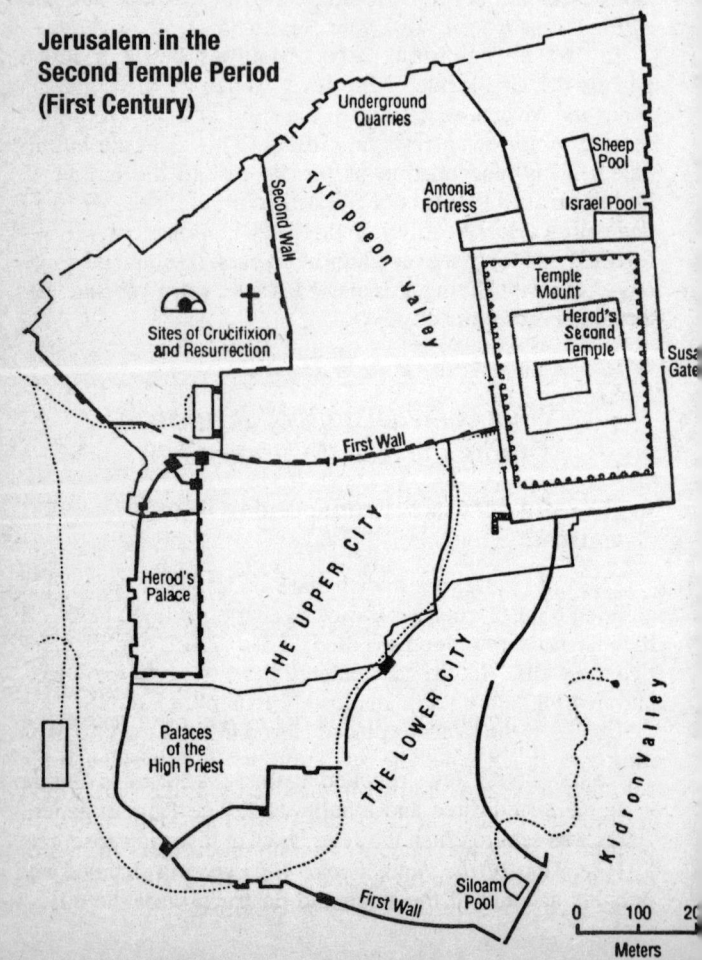

It was under Pontius Pilate's administration of Jerusalem that Jesus cleansed the Temple (John 2:14-16) and carried out his public ministry. It was in Jerusalem that Satan tempted Jesus (Matthew 4:5). Jerusalem was the city over which Jesus wept because of the spiritual blindness of its citizens and its upcoming destruction (Luke 19:41-44). Jesus also prophesied Jerusalem's yet future destruction during the tribulation (Matthew 24:4-28). Jesus prophesied that his death would occur in this city (Matthew 16:21; 20:17,18; Luke 9:31; 13:33). Finally, it was from the Mount of Olives, just east of Jerusalem that Jesus ascended into heaven (Acts 1:9,12) and it is to Jerusalem that Jesus will return at the second coming (Revelation 19:11-16).

8. What did Jesus prophesy about Jerusalem?

Jesus prophesied the destruction of Jerusalem which occurred in A.D. 70 (Luke 19:41-44), and also its future destruction during the tribulation (Matthew 24:1-31; Mark 13). He wept because of the unbelief of the city's inhabitants, and he clearly foretold of the devastation that was and is yet to come upon the great city. He knew that Jerusalem was strategic in biblical prophecy, but he also grieved for those within its walls. This is a great lesson for us as we study prophecy and its fulfillment. We can be certain that God's prophetic plan will be completed and at the same time, we can be sensitive to, and concerned for, those who have not accepted salvation. Indeed, the divine triumph of prophetic fulfillment will, for the unsaved, be a personal and eternal tragedy.

9. Why was Jerusalem destroyed in A.D. 70?

Daniel 9:26 prophesied not only the death of Jesus the Messiah, but also the destruction of Jerusalem which took place in A.D. 70. This was the third prophecy to be fulfilled regarding judgment on the city. The first was the destruction of the city and the temple by Nebuchadnezzar. The second was the desecration of the temple by Antiochus Epiphanes. The third was the prophecy of Jerusalem's complete destruction and its fulfillment.

In A.D. 66 the Jews revolted against the Romans and the struggle lasted three and a half years. The Roman general Titus was sent to crush the Jews. Jewish historian Josephus, in *The Wars of the Jews, books 4–6,* gives a detailed and graphic account of the siege and destruction of the city. A

Roman sympathizer, Josephus was present during the siege and even urged his fellow countrymen to surrender.[4] Eventually, the siege, its accompanying famine, and the breaching of the walls by the Romans led to the fall of the city. After several months, late in the summer of A.D. 70, the last of the Jews capitulated and Jerusalem fell. In Book 6.404–6, Josephus recorded the fate of those remaining under the sword of the Romans:

> Pouring into the alleys, sword in hand, they massacred indiscriminately all whom they met, and burnt the houses with all who had taken refuge within. Often in the course of their raids, on entering the houses for loot, they would find whole families dead and the rooms filled with victims of the famine, and then, shuddering at the sight, retire empty-handed. Yet, while they pitied those who had thus perished, they had no similar feelings for the living, they choked the alleys with corpses and deluged the whole city with blood, insomuch that many of the fires were extinguished by the gory stream.[5]

Upon entering the city, Titus was amazed at the Jewish fortifications and declared that the Roman victory was due to divine intervention.[6] He then ordered the destruction and razing of the entire city (except for a portion of the wall and towers), including the temple. With its destruction complete, biblical prophecy was once again fulfilled. The city into which Jesus made his triumphal entry was now memories and rubble. The words Jesus prophesied in Luke 19:41-44 were a reality:

> And when He approached, He saw the city and wept over it, saying, "If you had known in this day, even you, the things which make for peace! But now they have been hidden from your eyes. For the days shall come upon you when your enemies will throw up a bank before you, and surround you, and hem you in on every side, and will level you to the ground and your children within you, and they will not leave in you one stone upon another, because you did not recognize the time of your visitation."

Biblical scholar Dr. Harold Foos writes:

> Thus Jerusalem lay in ruins and desolation. The prophesied people had come against her. The promised destruction of the city and glorious Temple

had taken place. Her inhabitants were either dead or dispersed far from the glorious holy mountain. A deadly calm had settled over Zion. And over it all, as an epitaph, were the sorrowing words of Christ.[7]

"O Jerusalem, Jerusalem, *the city* that kills the prophets and stones those sent to her! How often I wanted to gather your children together, just as a hen *gathers* her brood under her wings, and you would not *have it!* Behold, your house is left to you *desolate;* and I say to you, you shall not see Me until *the time* comes when you say, 'Blessed *is* He who comes in the name of the Lord!' " (Luke 13:34-35).

PART 3

What Is the History of Jerusalem After the First Century?

10. What happened to the city during the early centuries of Christianity?

Although Jerusalem, in fulfillment of prophecy, had been destroyed in A.D. 70, the Romans rebuilt the city in A.D. 135 as a colony and named it Aelia Capitolina. Historian Robert L Wilken writes:

> After the defeat of Bar Kochba in 135 C.E. [A.D] the Romans plowed over the city of Jerusalem. Following an ancient rite for the founding of a new city, they yoked an ox and a cow to a curved plow, traversed the future city's boundaries, and where the earth formed a furrow marked out the location of its walls.... Named after the emperor's family, Aelius, and the gods of the Mons Capitolinus in Rome, Jupiter Optimus Maximus, Juno, and Minerva, Aelia Capitolina was henceforth to be a Roman colony, displacing the ancient city of the Jews.
>
> Every effort was made to sever Jerusalem's ties with the past and to erase signs of the city's ancient glory seat of Jewish kings.... Stones from the Jewish temple were used to build the theater and to construct the city wall. The temple mount itself was turned into a Roman farm.[8]

Although the new city continued to remain under Roman control for nearly another 200 years, from a human perspective, it was a place of little contemporary significance. "The new Roman city became a side alley in history, while Caesarea dominated the province of Syria Palestina. The centre of the cosmos founded upon the rock of Mount Moriah appeared to be a speck of sand blown away by the scrocco of time."[9]

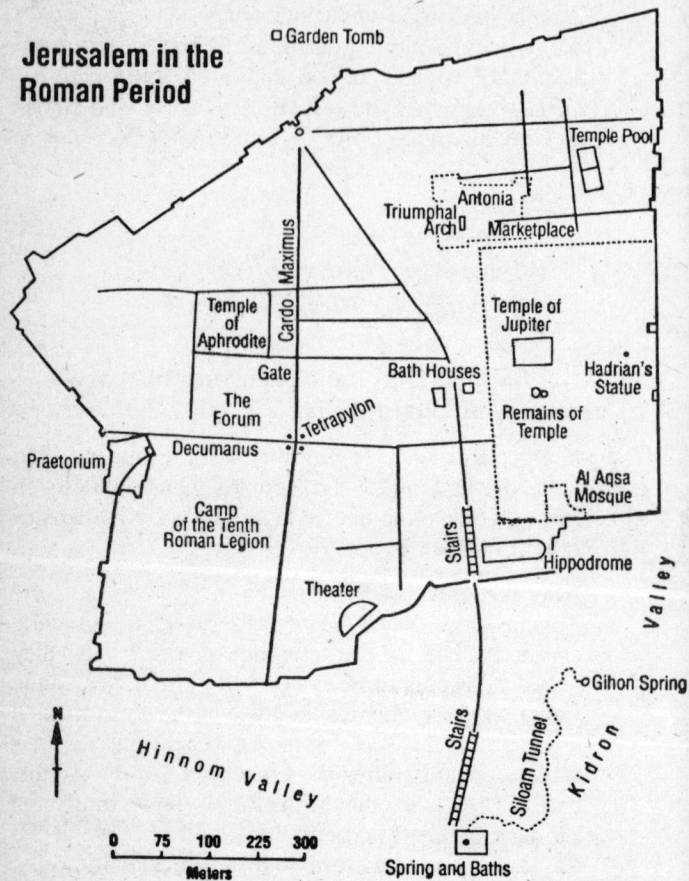

Jerusalem in the Roman Period

The Jews had been expelled from the city and were prohibited from entering it with the threat of death should they violate the ban. In the second and third centuries after Christ, Christianity began to develop in Aelia Capitolina (Jerusalem), and by the beginning of the fourth century (A.D. 300), Christian pilgrimages to the city began and there was some relaxing of the Jewish prohibition.[10]

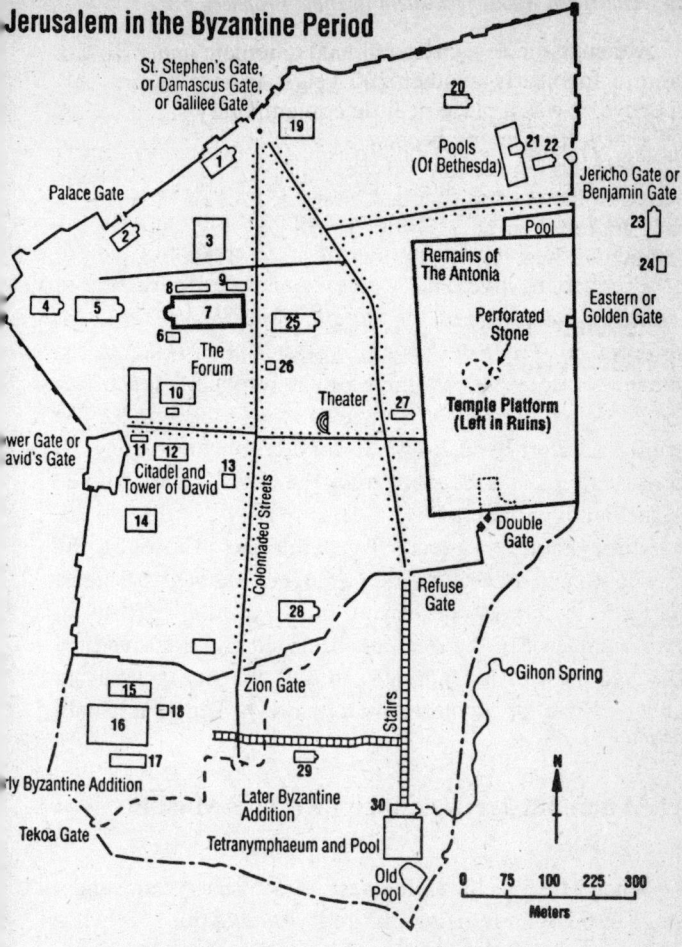

Jerusalem in the Byzantine Period

Churches and Other Religious Structures

1. Serapion Church
2. St. George's Church
3. Patriarch's Hospice or the Smith's Market
4. Theodorus Monastery
5. Spodaean Monastery
6. Baptistry
7. Church of the Holy Sepulchre
8. Priest's House
9. Patriarch's Palace
10. Greek Monastery Church John the Baptist
11. Monastery of St. Sabas
12. Iberian Monastery
13. Syrian Monastery
14. Church of St. James
15. House of Caiaphas
16. Basilica of Mt. Zion
17. St. Stephen's Church
18. Priest's House
19. Eudocia's Palace
20. Church of Mary Magdalene
21. Church of the Paralytic
22. Church of the Nativity of St. Mary
23. Tomb of the Virgin
24. Gethsemane
25. Church of SS Cosmos and Damianus
26. Home of the Aged
27. St. Sophia's Church
28. Nea (New) Church
29. Monastery of St. Peter
30. Eudocia's Church

When Constantine became ruler over Palestine in A.D. 324, the fortunes of Jerusalem once again came under the control and influence of Christendom. The emperor's mother, Helena, visited the city in 326 and a revived interest in alleged historic sites relating to Jesus and early Christianity occurred. This resurgence brought a renewal of the prohibition against the Jews, with the exception of the 9th of Av, when they were allowed to lament the destruction of the first two temples on the Temple Mount.[11]

From 361–363, the pagan emperor Julian (later called Julian the Apostate) attempted to reintroduce Græco-Roman religion, but also attempted to rebuild the temple. The effort was short-lived, however, for after only a few days of construction an earthquake struck the city and fires erupted in the building materials.[12]

Throughout Jerusalem's Byzantine era (330–638), the city continued under Christian influence although a Samaritan revolt in 529 destroyed much of the vicinity of Jerusalem. In 614 the Persians besieged and destroyed the city and most of its churches. In 629, the city came again under Byzantine control and remained "Christian" until 638.[13]

11. When did Jerusalem come under Muslim control?

When Muslims invaded Palestine, Jerusalem came under siege in 637 and remained so until March/April 638, when it surrendered to the Muslim Caliph Omar. From 638 until 1099, it remained firmly in Muslim control. Although the city was ruled by a number of Muslim leaders and many Arabs came to live in Jerusalem, the population remained predominately Christian. A limited number of Jews were allowed in the city.

In 691, the Muslim Caliph 'Abd al-Malik completed the Dome of the Rock on the Temple Mount (although it would not gain its reputation as the third holiest site in Islam until 1187 when the Crusaders were defeated by the Muslim leader Saladin).[14]

In 878, Jerusalem was annexed by Muslim powers in Egypt and with the exception of the Crusades, it remained under rulers from Cairo until the Ottoman conquest of

1516. Although under Muslim control during these centuries, Jerusalem was still subjected to war and destruction.

12. Why was Jerusalem important during the Crusades?

With the inauguration of the Crusades, Jerusalem became a focal point of Western history and a rallying point for Crusaders. In 1095 the Byzantine emperor Alexius I asked Pope Urban II for help in his struggle to regain territories lost in fighting with the Turks. Urban responded and the Crusades were initiated to retake by military force recently lost lands as well as other land, especially Jerusalem. "To the Crusaders, Jerusalem was both an actual and a visionary city, a walled place in Palestine and a paradise in the Holy Land."[15]

For a variety of reasons, some righteous, some unrighteous, but all sincere, European armies set out in the late eleventh century to recapture Jerusalem, Palestine, and the "Holy Land" so that it might once again come under Christian control. The primary tactical objective was the recapture of Jerusalem. The initial enthusiasm was high and the subsequent fighting was vicious. Arthur Sinclair wrote of these warriors:

> Without religious faith, few if any of the leading Crusaders would have set out, nor could they have recruited their barons and their knights and their foot soldiers without a fervent common conviction in their mission. Their task was in the service of God. The red cross sewn onto each surcoat and tunic was proof of divine protection as well as a mark for the Muslim enemy. This was to be the Army of Christ, with the Messiah riding in the heavens in front of the celestial hosts.... To the Crusaders, *Deus hoc vult* [God wills this]. The will of God would oversee their way.[16]

Jerusalem was besieged by the Crusaders from June 6 to July 15, 1099, when it was captured. It remained under Crusader control until 1187. In 1229, it came under attack from warriors of the Third Crusade who ruled it until 1244 when it fell to the Turks and later (1249) to the Egyptian Mamluks.

13. What happened to Jerusalem in the last few centuries?

For nearly 300 years Jerusalem remained under Egyptian control. From 1517, Jerusalem was under the rule of the Turkish Ottoman Empire. During these centuries of Muslim control, Jews and Christians were allowed to live in the city, but the major religious influence was that of Islam. During the 1800s the European powers began to once again look toward Jerusalem. England and France were especially interested in the Middle East and by the 1880s, the city was beginning to acquire the character of a "Western" city.[17]

PART 4

What Is the History of Jerusalem in the Present Century?

14. How did Jerusalem come under British control?

When World War I broke out in 1914, Jerusalem was still under control of the Turks. As the war progressed and Germany and its allies (including Turkey) began to suffer greater defeats, preparations were made by the Turks to evacuate Jerusalem. In December 1917 the city was evacuated and surrendered to British forces. For the next 30 years, until 1948, it remained under British rule.

15. What happened to Jerusalem when the state of Israel was created in 1948?

On May 14, 1948 independence was given to Israel and the state of Israel was founded. A year previously, in 1947, the United Nations had decided to partition Palestine into a Jewish and Arab state and had called for the "internationalization" of Jerusalem. Jewish authorities reluctantly accepted this plan, but the Arabs rejected it.[18] As a result, intense fighting broke out between Jewish and Arab forces in the two weeks after May 14, 1948. A cease-fire was proclaimed on June 11, 1948, leaving East Jerusalem under Arab control and West Jerusalem under Israeli control. For the next two decades, until June 1967, the city remained divided and subject to sporadic fighting and violence.[19]

16. What happened to Jerusalem during "The Six-Day War?"

The Six-Day War of June 1967 resulted in sweeping Israeli victories, including the capturing of East Jerusalem and the Old City which included the Temple Mount. However, as a goodwill gesture, control of the Temple Mount area including the Dome of the Rock was returned to Muslim religious authorities by Defense Minister Moshe Dayan ten days after its capture. With this one territorial exception, Jerusalem was once again, after almost 2000 years, a Jewish city under Jewish rule.

17. Is the current Israeli presence a fulfillment of biblical prophecy?

The Bible clearly teaches that the territory promised to Abraham (including Jerusalem) was promised unconditionally to the Jews.[20] If history is on the brink of the seven-year tribulation, then the current restoration of Israel and Jerusalem is the beginning of fulfillment of end-time Bible prophecy.

Belief in God's end-time plan, which revolves around national Israel, does not mean, as some critics claim, that we are insensitive to the human suffering and political difficulties surrounding Arab-Israeli affairs and Palestinian issues.[21] Rather, since we do not know precisely where we stand in history in relation to God's plan, we are attempting to faithfully, consistently, and accurately interpret and apply the Bible in all of its fullness.

18. How should Christians today view Jerusalem?

Jerusalem has a definite role in God's plan for the future. However, in our desire to interpret and apply biblical prophecy we should be careful in ascribing improper importance to any single contemporary event. Also, we should not give indiscriminate approval of or support to any and every action of the Israeli government. Our focus must remain firmly on the Scriptures and our standards for evaluating the actions of any person, government, or nation must be biblically-based. Our primary concern in this present age must be for the salvation of all people.

19. What are some of the major prophetic passages relating to Jerusalem?

While the Bible contains many prophecies about Jerusalem, some of the most extensive ones are found in Isaiah 60-61, Zechariah 12 and 14 and Revelation 21-22. These passages offer some of the clearest prophetic information about the city.

During the tribulation and the military campaign of Armageddon, Jerusalem will experience both peace and war. According to Daniel 9:27, after the first half of the tribulation the Antichrist will break the covenant of peace with Israel and intense persecution and suffering will occur in Jerusalem and throughout the world. This will culminate in the battle of Armageddon during which Jerusalem will be a focal point.

> "Behold, I am going to make Jerusalem a cup that causes reeling to all the peoples around; and when the siege is against Jerusalem, it will also be against Judah. And it will come about in that day that I will make Jerusalem a heavy stone for all the peoples; all who lift it will be severely injured. And all the nations of the earth will be gathered against it. In that day," declares the LORD, "I will strike every horse with bewilderment, and his rider with madness. But I will watch over the house of Judah, while I strike every horse of the peoples with blindness" (Zechariah 12:2-4).

At the end of the tribulation, at this critical time in Jerusalem's history and in all of human history, Jesus the Messiah will return to the Mount of Olives in Jerusalem and destroy his enemies which have assembled in military force at Armageddon. We read in Zechariah 14, especially verses 2-4 and 8-9:

> For I will gather all the nations against Jerusalem to battle, and the city will be captured, the houses plundered, the women ravished, and half of the city exiled, but the rest of the people will not be cut off from the city. Then the LORD will go forth and fight against

those nations, as when He fights on a day of battle. And in that day His feet will stand on the Mount of Olives, which is in front of Jerusalem on the east; and the Mount of Olives will be split in its middle from east to west by a very large valley, so that half of the mountain will move toward the north and the other half toward the south.... And it will come about in that day that living waters will flow out of Jerusalem, half of them toward the eastern sea and the other half toward the western sea; it will be in summer as well as in winter. And the LORD will be king over all the earth; in that day the Lord will be *the only* one, and His name *the only* one.

Also, when Jesus Christ returns, Jerusalem and Israel will acknowledge Him as the Messiah:

And I will pour out on the house of David and on the inhabitants of Jerusalem, the Spirit of grace and of supplication, so that they will look on Me whom they have pierced; and they will mourn for Him, as one mourns for an only son, and they will weep bitterly over Him, like the bitter weeping over a first-born (Zechariah 12:10).

Isaiah 60-61 describes the glory of Jerusalem and Israel during the millennium and the ministry of Jesus during this period. We read in Isaiah 60:14-15 of the great prestige of Jerusalem:

And the sons of those who afflicted you will come bowing to you, And all those who despised you will bow themselves at the soles of your feet; And they will call you the city of the LORD, The Zion of the Holy One of Israel. Whereas you have been forsaken and hated with no one passing through, I will make you an everlasting pride, A joy from generation to generation.

Additionally, the city will finally be a true city of peace, for God will "make peace your administrators, and righteousness your overseers. Violence will not be heard again in your land, nor devastation or destruction within your borders; But you will call your walls salvation, and your gates praise" (Isaiah 60:17d-18).

Isaiah continues to paint a picture of Zion's (i.e., Jerusalem) future during the thousand year reign of Messiah on earth from the Holy City. Even though Jerusalem has been the most conquered and destroyed city in the history of mankind, God's restoration and blessing to his beloved city will exceed the combined damage done throughout the ages. This reconstruction of Jerusalem will also bring religious and economic prosperity into her boundaries.

> Then they will rebuild the ancient ruins, they will raise up the former devastations, and they will repair the ruined cities, the desolations of many generations. And strangers will stand and pasture your flocks, and foreigners will be your farmers and your vinedressers. But you will be called the priests of the LORD; you will be spoken of *as* ministers of our God. You will eat the wealth of nations, and in their riches you will boast. Instead of your shame *you will have a* double *portion,* and instead of humiliation they will shout for joy over their portion. Therefore they will possess a double *portion* in their land, everlasting joy will be theirs. For I, the LORD, love justice, I hate robbery in the burnt offering; And I will faithfully give them their recompense, and I will make an everlasting covenant with them. Then their offspring will be known among the nations, and their descendants in the midst of the peoples. All who see them will recognize them because they are the offspring *whom* the LORD has blessed (Isaiah 61:4-9).

Revelation 21 and 22 describe Jerusalem during the millennium and in the eternal state. It will be a city of joy whose gates will never be closed. Ultimately it will be a city of purity inhabited only by believers.

> And in the daytime (for there shall be no night there) its gates shall never be closed; and they shall bring the glory and the honor of the nations into it; and nothing unclean and no one who practices abomination and lying, shall ever come into it, but only those whose

names are written in the Lamb's book of life (Revelation 21:25-27).

PART 5

What Is the Future of Jerusalem in the Tribulation?

20. Will Jerusalem be a city of peace or a city of war during this period?

Earlier we noted that Jerusalem will experience both war and peace during the tribulation. It has always been a city whose daily life swung as a pendulum between these two conditions. In the tribulation the pendulum will swing even faster. In the first half of the tribulation there will be peace in the city, although other disasters will befall it from the seal and trumpet judgments of Revelation 6, 8, and 9.

At some point during the tribulation, Israel will experience the fighting and events of Ezekiel 38-39, where armies from Gog and Magog will come against the nation. These forces will be destroyed by God through natural disaster and internal dissension (Ezekiel 38:17-23).

In the second half of the tribulation the city will experience war and fighting, especially at the end as the battle of Armageddon ensues. According to Zechariah 14:1-3, armies will be fighting in Jerusalem on the very day of the second coming of Christ. Zechariah writes:

> Behold, a day is coming for the LORD when the spoil taken from you will be divided among you. For I will gather all the nations against Jerusalem to battle, and the city will be captured, the houses plundered, the women ravished, and half of the city exiled, but the rest of the people will not be cut off from the city. Then the LORD will go forth and fight against those nations, as when He fights on a day of battle.

Under attack, Jerusalem will receive supernatural strength and the city will be victorious.

> "In that day the LORD will defend the inhabitants of Jerusalem, and the one who is feeble among them in

that day will be like David, and the house of David *will be* like God, like the angel of the LORD before them. And it will come about in that day that I will set about to destroy all the nations that come against Jerusalem" (Zechariah 12:8-9).

21. How does the Antichrist relate to the city?

During the tribulation there will be extensive political and religious activity in Jerusalem. We know from Daniel 9:24-27 that the Antichrist will make a political covenant with Israel. For the first three and a half years of the tribulation there will be some degree of political stability in Jerusalem and Israel, but this will eventually be shattered by the Antichrist as he transforms his image to include that of a religious leader.

At the mid-point of the tribulation the Antichrist will desecrate the temple, stop the worship in it, and begin to persecute the Jews in Jerusalem. This marks the beginning of the last half of the tribualtion and it is this that Jesus prophesied of in Matthew 24:15-22. At this time Jews living in Jerusalem are told to flee immediately from the city and go into the hills.

The Antichrist will be very active in the city and the fortunes of the city will turn from prosperity to persecution. It is reasonable to deduce from Scripture that the Antichrist will establish Jerusalem as his new capital. The Antichrist will be closely associated with the city, but that relationship will not endure and ultimately, Jerusalem will recognize the true Messiah.

22. What about the rebuilding of the temple in Jerusalem?

The first of two future temples will be rebuilt during the tribulation. The second, the Millennial Temple, will follow after the tribulation at the second coming. The existence of the Tribulation Temple is evidenced in passages such as Daniel 9:27; Matthew 24:15-16; 2 Thessalonians 2:3-4; and Revelation 11:1-2. This rebuilt temple will play a significant role in daily life and worship in Jerusalem and will help in preparing the nation for acceptance of Jesus as the Messiah and the second advent.[22]

23. What is the relationship of the "Two Witnesses" of Revelation 11 to the city?

According to Revelation 11:3-14, there will arise two unique witnesses proclaiming the gospel for a period of 1260 days during the tribulation. These two individuals, specially sealed by God to be a witness to Jerusalem and Israel, will arise probably during the first half of the tribulation. For three and a half years they will minister in Jerusalem without being harmed. At the end of the 1260 days, the Antichrist will kill them and their bodies will be left in the streets of Jerusalem for three and a half days after which God will resurrect them and rapture them to heaven. Once they have ascended to heaven, a great earthquake will occur, destroying a tenth of Jerusalem and killing 7000 people.

The two witnesses will be clothed in sackcloth (Revelation 11:3) which is symbolic of the fact that they are prophets of doom (cf. Isaiah 37:1-2; Daniel 9:3). While Jerusalem is not mentioned by name as the city of their ministry, Revelation 11:8 says that their dead bodies will lie "in the street of the great city which mystically is called Sodom and Egypt, where also their Lord was crucified." This reference to the crucifixion clearly places these two witnesses in Jerusalem. The reference to Sodom and Egypt implies that during this time there will be licentious behavior and Jewish persecution in the city. Regarding the ministries of these individuals, Dr. Foos observes:

> The significance of this particular prophecy concerning Jerusalem is singular. It indicates clearly that Jerusalem is not yet the holy city, the city of peace, that God promised it would be. The false Messiah and his counterfeit system will not bring in the promises that Israel has longed for. And despite the agonies experienced under the Antichrist and the direct judgments of God, the city does not yet turn to Jehovah but rather kills his messengers as it has always done.[23]

24. How does a revived Babylon affect the city?

Revelation 17 and 18 provide extensive prophecy regarding a "revived" Babylon during the tribulation. Most (though not all) prophecy scholars understand Revelation 17, especially verse 5, to be a symbolic reference to a worldwide religious movement. Chapter 18, however, is understood to refer to an economic or commercial center related to the contemporary site of the historic city of Babylon.[24]

Regardless of the specific identification of the city, its end is certain. At the end of the tribulation in conjunction with the battle of Armageddon, Babylon will be cataclysmically destroyed in a single day and hour just as happened in Daniel 5 by Darius (Revelation 18:8,10,17,19). Before its destruction Babylon will certainly affect tribulation life in Jerusalem, but unlike the latter, it will not exist after the second coming of Christ and in the millennium. The contrast is significant as Dr. Walvoord writes:

> As brought out in previous studies, because the destruction of Babylon was never consummated in history, though frequently prophesied in the Old Testament (Isa. 13-14; 21:9, 47; Jer. 50-51), a rebuilding of the city and its final destruction here would serve symbolically as well as practically for the majestic coming of Christ and as the end of the times of the Gentiles. The final world empire will be Roman as far as its political character is concerned, but spiritually it will correspond to Babylon with its false religion and its worship of Satan.[25]

25. What impact will the battle of Armageddon have on the city?

As noted earlier, Zechariah 14:1-3 tells us that there will be intense fighting in Jerusalem on the very day that the Lord Jesus returns at the second coming. Whether Armageddon will be a single battle or a campaign that encompasses even days or years, it will affect Jerusalem. Ultimately the security of the city will be assured by the return of Christ, but not before the city is attacked and many people flee from the city. Victory in Jerusalem is certain, but so is combat.

PART 6

What Is the Relationship of Jerusalem to the Second Coming?

26. Where does the Bible teach that Jesus will return to the Mount of Olives?

In the first chapter of Acts we read of the ascent of Jesus from the Mount of Olives after the resurrection and 40 days with the disciples. As the disciples stood watching the ascent, two angels appeared to them telling them that Jesus would return again to the same location, "and they also said, 'Men of Galilee, why do you stand looking into the sky? This Jesus, who has been taken up from you into heaven, will come in just the same way as you have watched Him go into heaven'" (Acts 1:11).

The return of Christ, or the second coming (not the rapture) was prophesied by Zechariah almost 600 years earlier in Zechariah 14:4: "And in that day His feet will stand on the Mount of Olives, which is in front of Jerusalem on the east; and the Mount of Olives will be split in its middle from east to west by a very large valley, so that half of the mountain will move toward the north and the other half toward the south." Because Christ delivered his great prophetic discourse on his second coming from the Mount of Olives, it is clearly implied that his return would be to the same location (Matthew 24-25).

Sixty years after the ascension, the Apostle John also wrote of Christ's second coming to earth in Revelation 19:11-16 although the Mount of Olives is not mentioned specifically. The second coming should not be confused with the rapture which occurs seven years earlier and is recorded in 1 Thessalonians 4:14-17. These two comings are quite separate and distinct events.[26]

27. Is the second coming different from the rapture?

It is after the rapture that the seven-year tribulation begins. The second coming of Christ then follows at the end of the tribulation. There are many passages differentiating the two events and numerous contrasts. At the rapture, Jesus does not return to Jerusalem or the earth but meets the Church in the air. At the second coming, Christ returns with the saints to the earth and Jerusalem as predicted in Zechariah 14:4-5 and Matthew 24:27-31.[27]

28. Why does Christ return to Jerusalem instead of some other city?

Christ will return to Jerusalem to judge the world and establish his millennial kingdom. He will also reign on the throne of David in fulfillment of Old Testament prophecies, which assured a Messiah-King for Israel from the Davidic line. While it will be a universal rule, it will be from Jerusalem because of the Davidic throne and the spiritual restoration of Israel. Dr. Walvoord writes:

> His reign over the house of Israel will be from Jerusalem (Isa. 2:1-4), and from the same location he will also reign as King of Kings and Lord of Lords over the entire earth (Ps. 72:8-11, 17-19).... The Millennium will be the occasion of the final restoration of Israel. At the beginning of the millennial kingdom Israel will experience her final and permanent regathering (Ezek. 39:25-29; Amos 9:15). Christ's reign over Israel will be glorious and will be a complete and literal fulfillment of all that God promised David (Jer. 23:5-8).[28]

No other city would permit the fulfillment of prophecy or allow for the rule and restoration of Israel. Jerusalem's biblical, prophetic, and worldwide significance will continue and be increased at the second coming of Christ.

PART 7

What Is the Future of Jerusalem in the Millennium?

29. What are the physical characteristics of the city during this time?

The Bible indicates in Zechariah 14:10 that after the battle of Armageddon the topography of Jerusalem and the surrounding area will be changed.

> All the land will be changed into a plain from Geba to Rimmon south of Jerusalem; but Jerusalem will rise

and remain on its site from Benjamin's Gate as far as the place of the First Gate to the Corner Gate, and from the Tower of Hananel to the king's wine presses.

The figure below depicts the configuration of Jerusalem during the millennium in relation to the rest of the land of Israel.

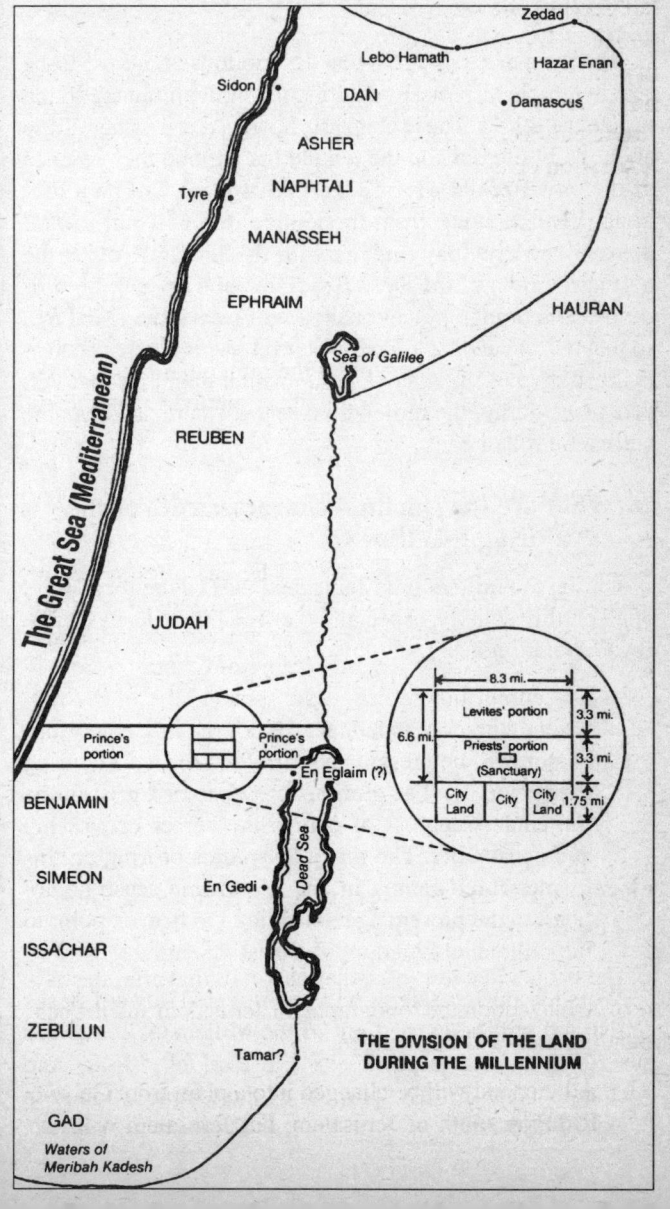

THE DIVISION OF THE LAND DURING THE MILLENNIUM

Dr. Walvoord writes of these changes:

> The effect of all the changes will be to elevate Jerusalem above the surrounding territory and to change the topography of Palestine to suit millennial conditions. This will accommodate therefore the temple of Ezekiel which would not fit Palestine in its present form.[29]

The most extensive physical descriptions of the yet-to-be rebuilt temple in Jerusalem during the millennium are found in Ezekiel 40-48. These chapters, however, tell us very little about daily life outside the temple but assume the presence of the city. Ezekiel 47:1-12 states that there will be a life-giving river flowing from the temple that will run toward the east and eventually merge with the Jordan River at the northern mouth of the Dead Sea (Ezekiel 47:6-12). Significantly, this topographical change will revive the Dead Sea so that it will become a fresh-water reservoir. Such a change is illustrative of the many environmental upgrades that will take place during the millennium as the Adamic and Noahic curses are rolled back.

30. What are the spiritual characteristics of the city during this time?

During the millennium, Jerusalem will be the focal point of all earthly activity, especially the worship of Jesus Christ. Dr. Walvoord notes:

> Of central importance in the spiritual life of the millennial kingdom is the fact that Christ in His glorious person will be present and visible in the world during the period.... The glorious presence of Christ in the millennial scene is of course the center of worship and spirituality. The many Scriptures bearing on this theme which cannot in any reasonable sense be applied to the present age nor limited to heaven point to the millennial kingdom of Christ on earth.[30]

Worship in Jerusalem will be directed toward Jesus Christ and will be carried out in the Millennial Temple as described in Jeremiah 33:15-22, Ezekiel 40-48, and Zechariah 14:16-21. The purpose of the temple is found in Ezekiel 37:26-28:

> "And I will make a covenant of peace with them; it will be an everlasting covenant with them. And I will place them and multiply them, and will set My sanctuary in their midst forever. My dwelling place also will be with them; and I will be their God, and they will be My people. And the nations will know that I am the LORD who sanctifies Israel, when My sanctuary is in their midst forever."

It is during these years that the new covenant spoken of in Jeremiah 31:31-37 and by Christ at the Last Supper will be fulfilled. Jeremiah declared:

> "But this is the covenant which I will make with the house of Israel after those days," declares the LORD, "I will put My law within them, and on their heart I will write it; and I will be their God, and they shall be My people. And they shall not teach again, each man his neighbor and each man his brother, saying, 'Know the LORD,' for they shall all know Me, from the least of them to the greatest of them," declares the LORD, "for I will forgive their iniquity, and their sin I will remember no more" (vv. 33-34).

Dr. Walvoord summarizes this time saying:

> Spiritual life in the millennium will be characterized by holiness and righteousness, joy and peace, the fullness of the Spirit, and the worship of the glorious Christ. The fact that Satan will be bound and demons will be inactive will provide a world scene in which spiritual life can abound.[31]

Throughout the world, but especially in Jerusalem, there will be peace, religious harmony, and united worship of Jesus Christ. In these days, Jerusalem will finally, truly be a city of peace as Isaiah prophesied:

> Now it will come about that In the last days, The mountain of the house of the LORD will be established as the chief of the mountains, And will be raised above the hills; And all the nations will stream to it. And many peoples will come and say, "Come, let us go up to the mountain of the LORD, To the house of the God of Jacob; That He may teach us concerning His ways, And that we may walk in His paths." For

the law will go forth from Zion, And the word of the Lord from Jerusalem. And He will judge between the nations, And will render decisions for many peoples; And they will hammer their swords into plowshares, and their spears into pruning hooks. Nation will not lift up sword against nation, And never again will they learn war (Isaiah 2:1-4).

31. What are the political characteristics of the city during this time?

Jesus Christ will establish a theocracy from Jerusalem and reign throughout the millennium. Beginning in Jerusalem there will be universal justice and peace (Isaiah 2:3-4; 11:2-5). Jeremiah recorded God's promises of this era that a Messiah-King would emerge from the Davidic dynasty and rule in righteousness and justice:

> In those days and at that time I will cause a righteous Branch of David to spring forth; and He shall execute justice and righteousness on the earth. In those days Judah shall be saved, and Jerusalem shall dwell in safety; and this is *the name* by which she shall be called: the Lord is our righteousness (Jeremiah 33:15-16).

For 1000 years Jerusalem will know peace and prosperity under the benevolent and righteous rule of Jesus Christ. All aspects of daily life will be affected as glory dwells in Immanuel's land from the Holy City.[32]

32. What happens to the city at the end of the millennium?

At the end of the millennium, Satan will be loosed and a final rebellion against God will ensue (Revelation 20:3,7-10). Satan and his forces will gather around Jerusalem in an attempt to capture it, but they are destroyed by God as fire comes from heaven to crush them. (The reference to Gog and Magog is not the same battle or the same people of Ezekiel 38-39.) After this event, there will be a time of final judgment (Revelation 20:11-15) and the final destruction of the earth by fire (Matthew 24:35; 2 Peter 3:10). The earthly city of Jerusalem will be consumed with the rest of the earth and will be replaced by a new city, the New Jerusalem (Revelation 3:12; 21:1-2).

PART 8

What Is the Future of Jerusalem in the Eternal State?

33. Why will the city continue to exist?

Apparently, God desires to carry forth the beloved name of Jerusalem as the name associated with his glory and presence. The New Jerusalem of Revelation 3:12 and 21-22 (also Hebrews 11:8-10; 12:22-25) will descend from heaven and continue through eternity. It will be the dwelling place of the redeemed of all ages who will serve God eternally (Revelation 22:3).

The Bible begins in the undeveloped setting of a garden, which man was supposed to develop. Instead, man rebels against God and is expelled from the garden and goes and builds a rebellious culture including his city, Babylon. However, Jesus Christ's intervention into history does finally result in proper dominion being exercised in eternity through the new humanity and as expressed in the development of a city—New Jerusalem.

34. What will be the size of the New Jerusalem?

Revelation 21:16-17 gives us clear dimensions of the New Jerusalem as 1,500 miles on every side, length, width, and height.

> And the city is laid out as a square, and its length is as great as the width; and he measured the city with the rod, fifteen hundred miles; its length and width and height are equal. And he measured its wall, seventy-two yards, *according* to human measurements, which are *also* angelic *measurements*.

If the New Jerusalem were present today, it would take up two-thirds of the continental United States, reaching from Maine to Florida, and from the Atlantic Seaboard to 600 miles west of the Mississippi River, stretching into the states of Nebraska and Kansas.

Differences arise as to the exact shape of the eternal city. David Cooper believed that the city would be a cube[33] as noted below.

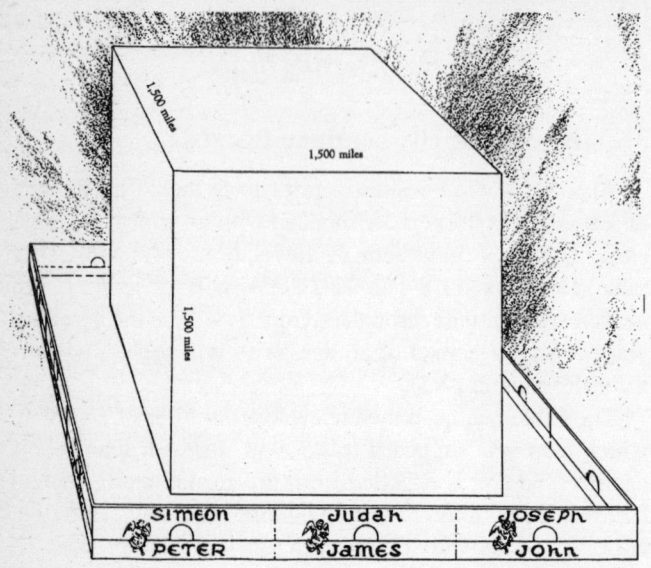

Clarence Larkin speculated that it would take the shape of a pyramid.[34]

Either way this city will differ from current cities because of its vertical dimension. Perhaps the vertical aspect reflects the harmony of heaven and earth during this era.

35. Will Jerusalem be an "earthly" city or a "heavenly" city during eternity?

Jesus told his disciples in John 14:2-3 that he was going away to heaven to prepare a place for believers. It appears that this place he is preparing is the Heavenly Jerusalem.

The New Jerusalem will be a heavenly city throughout eternity in that its origin is heavenly, as opposed to having been built upon this earth. However, it will be earthly, in that it is physical and geographical. It will be the earthly part of the new heavens and the new earth, which will replace the current heavens and earth after their destruction. After this present earth has been destroyed by fire (2 Peter 3:10), the new city will descend from the heavens.

> And I saw a new heaven and a new earth; for the first heaven and the first earth passed away, and there is no longer *any* sea. And I saw the holy city, new Jerusalem, coming down out of heaven from God, made ready as a bride adorned for her husband. And I heard a loud voice from the throne, saying, "Behold, the tabernacle of God is among men, and He shall dwell among them, and they shall be His people, and God Himself shall be among them" (Revelation 21:1-3).

Revelation 21-22 is very specific and detailed about the city, its inhabitants, and the blessedness of the eternal state. Though there are many questions we may have about eternity, John's vision leaves no doubt that citizens of this New Jerusalem, *the* eternal city, will exist in conditions unlike any this world has known.

36. Will there be other cities as well?

There is no mention of any other eternal city in the Bible and there is no reason to think that there might be other cities. Jerusalem alone has been a unique and divinely-appointed city throughout history. Its significance has not been and will not be duplicated or repeated. The Lake of Fire is not described in the Bible as a city.

PART 9

Why Does This Matter Today?

37. How do the prophecies concerning Jerusalem affect my daily life?

For most of us Jerusalem is far away, a dot on a map, or a photograph in *National Geographic*. Few of us will ever go there, and much less, live there. Yet its existence and future is important to the entire world because of the role it plays in history. As Christians, if we seriously want to understand, evangelize, and engage the world in which we live, we must understand God's plan for history.

Just as Paul encouraged Timothy writing "all Scripture is inspired by God and profitable for teaching, for reproof, for correction, for training in righteous" (2 Timothy 3:16), we too, live and believe the same. That which is true of all biblical prophecy, is true regarding Jerusalem and prophecy.

> Why study Bible prophecy? Is our goal to produce charts and graphs and to fill our heads with facts? If so, we are not using Bible prophecy the way God intended. God did share with us what will happen in the future, but He did so to change our lives. We ought to respond to prophecy with a sense of awe and wonder at the God of the universe who can announce what will take place and then bring it to pass. We ought to feel a sense of comfort and encouragement as we realize that the God who can work out the fate of nations also can work out the details of our lives. This should produce stability and maturity as we refuse to get upset by the circumstances in which we find ourselves. Finally, knowing what God is going to do should motivate us to live holy lives because someday we will stand before Him to give account.[35]

Even though our myopic focus may too often be on the "daily grind," when we reflect upon our eternal destiny from God's perspective, we must realize that the future of every believer is vitally linked to a city named Jerusalem. Not only is prophecy relevant, it is personal!

38. How should I pray for Jerusalem and the Middle East?

Journalists, diplomats, politicians, and historians frequently use the phrase "peace and prosperity." However, from a biblical perspective "peace and salvation" is correct. We should pray daily for peace in the Middle East so that the gospel and the message of Jesus Christ can spread unimpeded (1 Timothy 2:1-4). Recognizing God's prophetic plan, we should pray for peace throughout the region and for the salvation of all people that inhabit it.

The pain, pride, prejudice, and politics of the Middle East are very real. The suffering has been immense and the solutions are elusive. Yet, the prophecies are as real as the problems and the solution rests in the Scripture and the Savior.

As we await the return of Jesus Christ, Jerusalem's Messiah-King, we should read and heed the words of King David:

> Pray for the peace of Jerusalem: "May they prosper who love you. May peace be within your walls, And prosperity within your palaces." For the sake of my brothers and my friends, I will now say, "May peace be within you" (Psalm 122:6-8).

For this prayer to be finally answered, Jerusalem will first pass through her greatest time of trial and calamity in her long history. Peace will not come to Jerusalem until the second coming of Christ, which will follow the horrors and devastation of the seven-year tribulation. The peace of Jerusalem will come, but it will be preceded by much sorrow. Thus, in a sense, to pray for the peace of Jerusalem is to pray for a speedy culmination of God's plan which includes tribulation before peace.

39. Should or can Christians be Zionists?

Zionism was and is primarily a political movement. As Christians, during this current age, our *primary* focus with regard to Israel and Jerusalem should be the salvation of the Jews, not patriotism for Israelis. Evangelicals staunchly supported Zionist calls for a homeland in the decades before 1948 and have continued support of Israel since that time. This has been rightly grounded in an understanding of the unconditional promise of "the land" to Abraham. While affirming this interpretation, we must apply it carefully. The *unqualified* merging of politics, nationalism, and the Bible is an extreme to be avoided regardless of the nation involved, be it Israel, the United States, or any other nation. We need to be informed about the world around us and we need to call the world to biblical standards and biblical principles. We should pray for all Christians in the Middle East and support a resolution of the many issues of the region.

Politics in the Middle East are volatile and complex.[36] For Christians to uncritically support contemporary political Israel simply because of the priority of Israel in the Bible and prophecy is wrong. Our support must be conditional, biblically grounded, and informed. This is illustrated in our relationship with our own country. We support the nation but may often disagree with various policies generated by certain entities who control the government. So also we must be willing to distinguish God's chosen people, the Jews, from the present State of Israel when necessary. The former must always have our support, but not so with the latter. The former is unconditional, the latter is conditional.

40. Isn't this really all just speculation?

Amos Elon, one of Israel's most prominent writers, is certainly correct when he writes that, "the rational mind has always had reservations about Jerusalem."[37] This is due in part to the spiritual significance of the city from both human and divine perspectives. Jerusalem is not "just another city." The prophecies concerning its future are just as certain as other biblcal prophecies, many of which have already been fulfilled. All interpretations of prophecy are subject to error but that does not invalidate the prophecy, just the interpretation. This is not, however, an excuse for us to ignore prophetic literature and diligent study of God's Word. The hundreds of references to Jerusalem in the Bible are there for a reason. The responsibility is ours to accurately handle the word of truth (2 Timothy 2:15).

Conclusion

More than two dozen times in its 3000-year history Jerusalem has been besieged, plundered, and conquered. A list of those who have conquered it, ruled it, or attempted to rule it and affect its destiny reads like a Who's Who of history. Yet, none of these figures is nearly as important as the One who will ultimately rule. The appeal of Jerusalem through the centuries has been multi-dimensional. It has counted among its inhabitants prophets, priests, pilgrims, potentates, and patriots. It has attracted the righteous and the unrighteous, saints and sinners. Yet one day it will claim as its citizens the redeemed of all ages who will eternally worship their Lord, for,

> there shall no longer be any curse; and the throne of God and of the Lamb shall be in it, and His bond-servants shall serve Him; and they shall see His face, and His name shall be on their foreheads. And there shall no longer be any night; and they shall not have need of the light of a lamp nor the light of the sun, because the Lord God shall illumine them; and they shall reign forever and ever (Revelation 22:3-5).

Appendix: Is the Heavenly Jerusalem present during the millennium?

Some biblical scholars and prophecy students who have studied the future of Jerusalem have disagreed over the location of the Heavenly Jerusalem during the millennium. Some believe that it will remain in heaven until the beginning of the eternal state. Others think that it will be present during the millennium, hovering above earthly Jerusalem and will be the abode of resurrected believers.

While most agree that Revelation 21 and 22 describe the heavenly Jerusalem, some interpret the passage as descriptive of Jerusalem during the millennium. Others see it as descriptive of Heavenly Jerusalem during the eternal state. There is also a mediating position which sees these verses as describing the eternal habitation of resurrected saints during the millennium and continuing into the eternal state.

Following this mediating position, Dr. J. Dwight Pentecost writes:

> When the occupants of the city are described it must be seen that they are in their eternal state, possessing their eternal inheritance, in eternal relationship with God who has tabernacled among them. There will be no change in their position or relation whatsoever.

When the occupants of the earth are described they are seen in the millennial age. They have an established relationship to the heavenly city which is above them, in whose light they walk. Yet their position is not eternal nor unchangeable, but rather millennial.[38]

Regardless of the view taken regarding the possibility of a "heavenly Jerusalem" which hovers over the earth during the millennium and in which those individuals with resurrection bodies dwell, Scripture is clear that there will be an earthly city of Jerusalem and a new Heavenly Jerusalem. Just when the Heavenly Jerusalem will make its appearance in history is the question under discussion. All agree that both are a part of God's plan for history.

A Brief Chronology of Jerusalem

B.C. (also B.C.E.)

ca. 2000–1600	—	Known as Urushalim
ca. 1390–1003	—	Occupied by Jebusites
1004	—	David conquers and fortifies the city (Joshua 15:63; 1 Chronicles 11:5)
1004–970	—	David reigns in Jerusalem
996	—	David makes Jerusalem his capital
966–959	—	Solomon constructs first temple
597	—	Captured by Babylonian king, Nebuchadnezzar
587	—	Destroyed by Nebuchadnezzar
515	—	Consecration of rebuilt temple by Zerubbabel ("Second Temple")
332	—	Alexander the Great gains control of Jerusalem from Persians
323	—	Antigonus gains control
301–200	—	Under control of Ptolomies
198	—	Conquered by Antiochus
175–164	—	Ruled by Antiochus IV (Antiochus Epiphanes)
168	—	Antiochus desecrates the altar in the temple
167–63	—	Revolt of the Maccabees and under Hasmonean control
63	—	Conquered by Roman general Pompey
40	—	Plundered by Parthians from Persia
37–4	—	Herod appointed king by Rome
20	—	Reconstruction of Temple begins
5/4 (winter)	—	Birth of Jesus in Bethlehem
4 B.C.–6 A.D.	—	Ruled by Herod's son, Archelaus

A.D. (also C.E.)

6–41	—	Ruled by Roman procurators (by Pontius Pilate 26–36)
33 (March)	—	Triumphal entry by Jesus
41–44	—	Ruled by Herod Agrippa
44–66	—	Ruled by Roman procurators
66–70	—	Jewish revolt

70	—	Jerusalem destroyed by Roman general Titus
70–330	—	***Roman control***
135	—	Rebuilt as the Roman colony Aelia Capitolina
330–638	—	***Byzantine control***
614	—	Captured and sacked by Persians
638–1099	—	***Arab control***
638	—	Conquered by Arabs
692	—	Dome of the Rock completed
1099	—	Besieged and conquered by Christians of the First Crusade
1099–1187	—	***Crusader control***
1187	—	Conquered by Muslim forces under Saladin
1187–1229	—	***Arab control***
1219	—	Walls razed by Malik al-Muazzam Isa
1229–1244	—	***Crusader control***
1244–1260	—	***Arab control***
1260	—	Conquered by Mongols and retaken by Mamluks
1260–1516	—	***Arab control***
1516	—	Ottoman conquest
1517–1917	—	***Under Ottoman rule***
1542	—	Turkish sultan Suleiman the Magnificent rebuilds city walls seen today
1831	—	Egyptian occupation
1840	—	Reoccupation by Turks
1917 (December 9)	—	Surrendered by Turks to British
1917–1948	—	***British control***
1921–1936	—	Arab riots and uprisings
1948–1967	—	***Jordanian control***
1967	—	***Israeli control***
1987–1993	—	Palestinian uprising ("Intifada")
1994	—	Israeli-Jordanian peace treaty
1996	—	Trimillennium anniversary celebration

Notes

1. Eugene Merrill, Kingdom of Priests: A History of Old Testament Israel (Grand Rapids: Baker Book House, 1987), pp. 234–36, 43–48.

2. Harold W. Hoehner, *Chronological Aspects of the Life of Christ* (Grand Rapids: Zondervan Publishing House, 1977), p. 126.

3. Ibid., p. 138.

4. Josephus, *Wars of the Jews* 5.371. See also Cleon L. Rogers, Jr., *The Topical Josephus* (Grand Rapids: Zondervan Publishing House, 1992), pp. 156–204 for a summary of the siege and destruction.

5. Josephus, *Wars of the Jews* 6.404–6.

6. Ibid., 6.411–13.

7. Harold David Foos, "Jerusalem in Prophecy" (Th.D. dissertation, Dallas Theological Seminary, 1965), p. 209.

8. Robert L. Wilken, *The Land Called Holy* (New Haven, CT: Yale University Press), pp. 82–83.

9. Andrew Sinclair, *Jerusalem: The Endless Crusade* (New York: Crown Publishers, 1955), p. 13.

10. *Encyclopedia Judaica,* "Jerusalem," p. 1406.

11. Ibid.

12. For a full account of this attempt at rebuilding the temple, see Jeffrey Brodd, "Julian the Apostate and His Plan to Rebuild the Jerusalem Temple," *Bible Review* 11 (October 1995): 32–38, 48.

13. *Encyclopedia Judaica,* "Jerusalem," p. 1407–08.

14. Thomas Ice and Randall Price, *Ready to Rebuild: The Imminent Plan to Rebuild the Last Days Temple* (Eugene, OR: Harvest House, 1992), pp. 85–93. The dates surrounding the construction and proclamation of the site as holy will become very significant in later controversy regarding the Temple Mount. That significance remains today.

15. Sinclair, *Jerusalem,* p. 36.

16. Ibid., pp. 45–46.

17. *Encyclopedia Judaica,* "Jerusalem," p. 1459.

18. Ibid., p. 1477.

19. Ibid., p. 1483.

20. Paul N. Benware, *Understanding End Times Prophecy: A Comprehensive Approach* (Chicago: Moody Press, 1995), pp. 34–57.

21. Cf. Na'im Ateek, "Jerusalem in Islam and for Palestinian Christians with Postscript" in P.W.L. Walker, ed., *Jerusalem Past and Present in the Purposes of God,* 2nd ed. (Grand Rapids: Baker Book House, 1994), p. 153.

22. See in this same series, *The Truth About the Last Day's Temple* (Eugene, OR: Harvest House, 1996) and Thomas Ice and Randall Price,

Ready to Rebuild: The Imminent Plan to Rebuild the Last Days Temple (Eugene, OR: Harvest House, 1992).

23. Foos, "Jerusalem in Prophecy," p. 241.

24. Charles H. Dyer, *World News and Bible Prophecy* (Wheaton, IL: Tyndale House, 1993), pp. 141–52. By the same author and publisher, see also *The Rise of Babylon: Sign of the End Times,* 1991.

25. John F. Walvoord, *Major Bible Prophecies: 37 Crucial Prophecies that Affect You Today* (Grand Rapids: Zondervan Publishing House, 1991), pp. 358–59.

26. Thomas Ice and Timothy Demy, *The Truth About the Rapture* (Eugene, OR: Harvest House, 1996), pp. 26–33.

27. Ibid.

28. Walvoord, *Major Bible Prophecies,* pp. 390, 391.

29. John F. Walvoord, *The Millennial Kingdom* (Findlay, OH: Dunham Publishing Co., 1959), p. 321.

30. Walvoord, *Millennial Kingdom,* pp. 306–07.

31. Ibid., p. 315.

32. For a fuller discussion by the authors, see in this same series, *The Truth About the Millennium* (Eugene, OR: Harvest House, 1996).

33. David L. Cooper, *The World's Greatest Library: Graphically Illustrated* (Los Angeles: Biblical Research Society, 1970), p. 107.

34. Clarence Larkin, *The Book of Revelation Illustrated* (Philadelphia: Clarence Larkin Estate, 1919), p. 204.

35. Dyer, *World News,* pp. 279–80.

36. For a good summary see David A. Rausch, *The Middle East Maze: Israel and Her Neighbors* (Chicago: Moody Press, 1991).

37. Amos Elon, *Jerusalem: Battlegrounds of Memory* (New York: Kodansha International, 1995), p. 238.

38. J. Dwight Pentecost, *Things to Come: A Study in Biblical Eschatology* (Grand Rapids: Zondervan Publishing House, 1958), p. 580.

Recommended Reading

Benware, Paul N. *Understanding End Times Prophecy: A Comprehensive Approach.* Chicago: Moody Press, 1995.

Dyer, Charles H. *The Rise of Babylon: Sign of the End Times.* Wheaton, IL: Tyndale House, 1991.

―――――. *World News and Bible Prophecy.* Wheaton, IL: Tyndale House, 1991.

Elon, Amos. *Jerusalem: Battlegrounds of Memory.* New York: Kodansha International, 1995.

Foos, Harold David. "Jerusalem in Prophecy." Th.D. dissertation. Dallas Theological Seminary, 1965.

Hoehner, Harold W. *Chronological Aspects of the Life of Christ.* Grand Rapids: Zondervan Corporation, 1977.

Hunt, Dave. *Cup of Trembling: Jerusalem and Bible Prophecy.* Eugene, OR: Harvest House, 1995.

Ice, Thomas and Randall Price, *Ready to Rebuild: The Imminent Plan to Rebuild the Last Days Temple.* Eugene, OR: Harvest House, 1992.

Larsen, David L. *Jews, Gentiles, and the Church: A New Perspective on History and Prophecy.* Grand Rapids: Discovery House Publishers, 1995.

Merrill, Eugene. *Kingdom of Priests: A History of Old Testament Israel.* Grand Rapids: Baker Book House, 1987.

Pentecost, J. Dwight. *Things to Come: A Study in Biblical Eschatology.* Grand Rapids: Zondervan Publishing House, 1958.

Rausch, David A. *The Middle East Maze: Israel and Her Neighbors.* Chicago: Moody Press, 1991.

Rogers, Cleon Jr. *The Topical Josephus.* Grand Rapids: Zondervan Publishing House, 1992.

Sinclair, Andrew. *Jerusalem: The Endless Crusade.* New York: Crown Publishers, 1955.

Tan, Paul Lee. *The New Jerusalem.* Rockville, MD: Assurance Publishers, 1978.

Walvoord, John F. *Major Bible Prophecies: 37 Crucial Prophecies that Affect You Today.* Grand Rapids: Zondervan Publishing House, 1991.

―――――. *The Millennial Kingdom.* Findlay, OH: Dunham Publishing Co., 1959.

Wilken, Robert L. *The Land Called Holy.* New Haven, CT: Yale University Press, 1992.